759.949 J35j
JANSSENS
 JAMES ENSOR

FV

9.95

WITHDRAWN

JAMES ENSOR

JAMES ENSOR

by Jacques Janssens

CROWN PUBLISHERS, INC. - NEW YORK

Title page: SELF-PORTRAIT IN A FLOWERED HAT, 1883
Oil on canvas, 29½" × 24¼" (75 × 61,5 cm.)
Stedelijk Museum, Ostend

Collection published under the direction of:
MADELEINE LEDIVELEC-GLOECKNER

PHOTOGRAPHS

A.C.L., Brussels – Henry Beville, Annapolis, Md. – J. Blauel, Gauting Munich – Clichés Musées Nationaux, Paris – E. Dulière, Brussels – t'Felt, Antwerp – J. Hyde, Paris – Otto Nelson, New York – Raf van den Abele, Gent – Studio Reto, Gstaad – Joseph Szaszfai, New Haven, Conn.

We wish to thantk the owners of the pictures by James Ensor reproduced in this book:

MUSEUMS

Koninklijk Museum voor Schone Kunsten, Antwerp – Plantin-Moretus Museum, Antwerp – Musées Royaux des Beaux-Arts de Belgique, Brussels – Museum voor Schone Kunsten, Ghent – Musée des Beaux-Arts, Liège – Stedelijk Museum, Ostend – Musée national d'art moderne, Centre Georges Pompidou, Paris – Musée Wallraf-Richartz, Cologne – Bayerische Staatsgemäldesammlungen, Munich – Staatsgalerie, Stuttgart – Art Institute, Chicago – Minneapolis Institute of Arts – Museum of Modern Art, New York – Yale University Art Gallery, New Haven, Conn.

GALLERY

Le Bateau-Lavoir, Paris.

PRIVATE COLLECTIONS

Mr. and Mrs. James W. Alsdorf, Chicago – Barbara Meyer Elesh, U.S.A. – Louis Franck, Esq., C.B.E. Gstaad – Georges de Graeve, Brussels – Marcel Mabille, Brussels – Mr. and Mrs. Herman D. Shickman, New York.

Library of Congress Cataloging in Publication Data
Janssens, Jacques.
    Ensor.
    Bibliography: p. 94–95

    1. Ensor, James, baron, 1860–1949. 2. Painters–
Belgium–Biography.
ND673.E6J3613   759.9493 [B]   78–9884
ISBN 0–517–53284–0

PRINTED IN ITALY – © 1978 BY BONFINI PRESS CORPORATION, NAEFELS, SWITZERLAND
ALL RIGHTS FOR REPRODUCTION OF ILLUSTRATIONS BY S.P.A.D.E.M., PARIS
ALL RIGHTS IN THE U.S.A. ARE RESERVED BY CROWN PUBLISHERS, INC., NEW YORK, N.Y.

RED APPLES AND WHITE BOWL, 1883   Oil on canvas, 23⅝″ × 29½″ (60 × 75 cm.)   Private collection

A ROAD WITH MANY TURNINGS

James Ensor is known to the public as a painter of masks and skeletons. This is true to such an extent that his masquerades and macabre figures sometimes cause one to forget that he did a great many other things — that he was very much more than that. Yet the unusual and the fantastic constitute only one of the many aspects of his work, whose principal virtue is its exceptional diversity. Few painters have been capable of achieving greater variety in their art than he, of finding renewed inspiration and fresh forms, of intensifying their experimentation and adventuring into unexplored territories, each one very different from the other. A multifaceted artist, curious about everything, prodigiously inventive, of unparalleled boldness, and a man ahead of his time, this innovator, whose imagination was incredibly fertile, tried every kind of artistic endeavor and expressed himself in many ways, invariably displaying a stunning originality.

The multiplicity of his ideas and the eclecticism of his compositions can be explained by the painter's origins and environment. He was clearly a product of the rich Flemish earth, the earth

Ensor Drawing, 1885
Pencil, 8⅝" × 6¾" (22 × 17 cm.)
Collection: Marcel Mabille, Brussels

which cradled him, in which he took root and which nourished him from the beginning to the end of his long career. The Flemish spirit, along with all of those characteristics and shadings which are its special properties, inspired his creations and permeated all of them.

The Flemish spirit is positive, realistic in its outlook, sees things as they are. Thus Ensor's work is realistic and naturalistic, his subjects are men and women of the people, and his portraits are rich in psychological analyses and imposing in their truthfulness. The Flemish spirit is partial to an ambience that is intimate, quiet, and tranquil. Thus we have interior scenes, discrete evocations of the middle-class society of the period. The Flemish spirit is dreamy, turning its eyes to far horizons and sensitive to plays of light and the kinship of colors. Thus we have seascapes and landscapes bathed in a vibrant luminosity. The Flemish spirit is mystical and religious. Thus we have episodes in the life of Christ interpreted very freely but with obvious reverence. The Flemish spirit savors the products of the earth and the sea and also the riches of nature. Thus we have still lifes of an exquisite sensuality set off by subtle coloring. The Flemish spirit delights in heavy-handed jokes and hearty laughter. And so we have satirical paintings and humorous cartoons which, we must admit, never rise to a very high level. Finally, the Flemish spirit is attracted by the miraculous and the supernatural and likes to regale itself with old legends

6

Self-Portrait, 1883
Pencil, 8¹³/₁₆″ × 7¹/₂″ (22,5 × 19 cm.)
Collection: Marcel Mabille, Brussels

and fantastic tales. And thus we have the familiar phantasmagoria of carnival masks and skeletons that look as if they might have escaped from some «danse macabre» of the Middle Ages.

These canvases, inspired by such different and sometimes contradictory concerns, cannot be classified according to periods. The painter did not produce them in any logical order, but capriciously as the mood struck him. He can be seen producing at the same time pictures whose tones and styles are entirely the reverse of one another, at every turn going from one sort of picture to another, returning to a source of inspiration which has been temporarily abandoned and then abruptly setting out again toward new horizons and over and over again changing course with disarming spur-of-the-moment casualness. In his work subjects and forms of expression exist alongside each other and, one might say, elbow and jostle one another, while, paradoxically, the very disparity between the elements in the pictures somehow manages to effect a harmonious whole.

This diversity gives particularly appealing originality to works which are constantly wandering over the artistic landscape and establishing new frontiers. This work is a conglomeration of fresh personal vision, unceasing experimentation, incessant renewals, surprising inventiveness, unexpected leaps forward, and an inextricable crisscrossing of categories and styles. Inevitably, this

A Gust of Wind at the Edge of the Forest, 1888   Etching, 6⅝″ × 9⅜″ (16,6 × 23,8 cm.)
Art Institute of Chicago. Print and Drawing Fund

diversity makes analysis difficult. It is impossible to classify the painter as belonging to any particular school. One cannot attach a label to an artist who has tried everything, done everything, expressed everything, and who has shown a propensity to use different techniques, simultaneously or successively, without consistently employing any one of them, without belonging to any school, without a commitment to any specific system of esthetics. Even the steps in his evolution are hard to follow. One can point out stages of his development, yet still not be able to see the whole picture of the meandering road he has taken. Thus Ensor occupies a unique place in the history of painting.

How to explain this artist, whose genius was so many-sided and so unbridled? How to read his motives and discern what secret sources fed his inspiration? His personality was complex, of a complexity at odds with the even tenor of an uneventful life. He reveals himself as having been at once tragic and satirical, bitter and mischievous, realistic and idealistic, tormented and enthusiastic. An ever-changing turn of mind set the tone, which varied from picture to picture, of each canvas produced by his brush. He was also a wide-awake dreamer. Dreams played an important role in his life. It pleased him to transpose them onto his work.

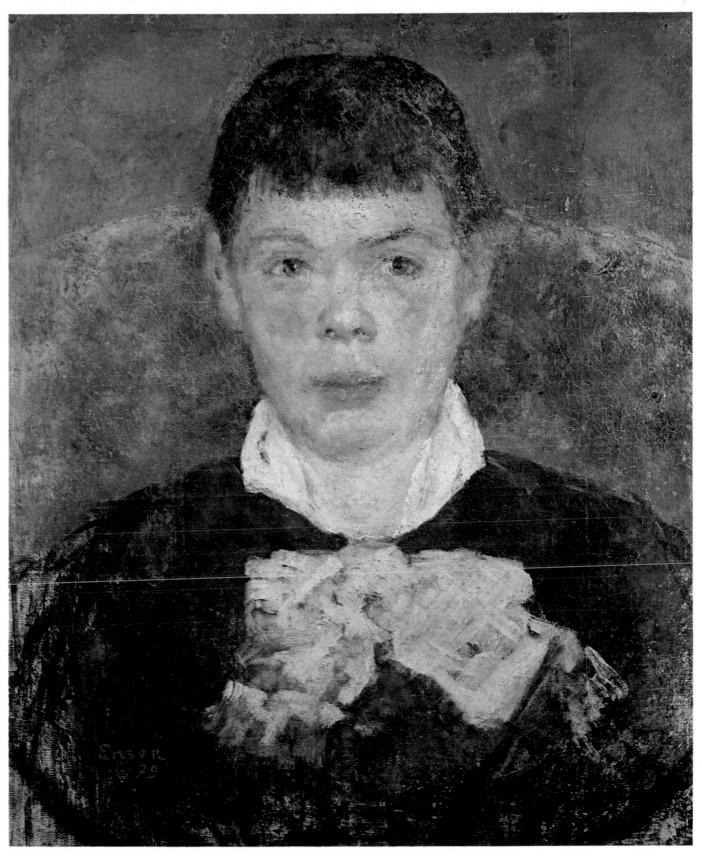

WOMAN WITH TURNED-UP NOSE, 1879   Oil on canvas, 21¼″ × 17¹¹⁄₁₆″ (54 × 45 cm.)
Koninklijk Museum voor Schone Kunsten, Antwerp

THE LAMP BOY,
1880
Oil on canvas,
59½″ × 35⅞″
(151 × 91 cm.)
Musées Royaux des
Beaux-Arts de Belgique,
Brussels
◁

▷
THE SOMBER LADY,
1881
Oil on canvas,
39¼″ × 31⅞″
(100 × 81 cm.)
Musées Royaux des
Beaux-Arts de Belgique,
Brussels

VLAANDERENSTRAAT IN THE SNOW, 1880   Oil on canvas, 18⅞″ × 11⅞″ (47,9 × 28,4 cm.)
Collection: Louis Franck, Esq., C.B.E. Gstaad

AFTERNOON AT OSTEND, 1881   Oil on canvas, 42½″ × 52⅜″ (108 × 133 cm.)
Koninklijk Museum voor Schone Kunsten, Antwerp

14   Portrait of the Artist's Father, 1881   Oil on canvas, 39¼″ × 31⅞″ (100 × 81 cm.)
Musées Royaux des Beaux-Arts de Belgique, Brussels

PORTRAIT OF THE ARTIST'S MOTHER, 1881   Oil on canvas, 39¼″ × 31½″ (100 × 80 cm.)   15
Musées Royaux des Beaux-Arts de Belgique, Brussels

16 RUSSIAN MUSIC, 1881   Oil on canvas, 52⅜″ × 43″ (133 × 110 cm.)
Musées Royaux des Beaux-Arts de Belgique, Brussels

A substantial part of his output, in fact, was a projection of his dreams. At other times his pictures were just playful. In both instances they represented a break with reality, an excursion into an airy universe where all was imagination, poetry, light, and color.

The artist himself stated: «Ensor changes his style as if he were changing shirts.» However, whatever he does he remains the same, true to himself. The style of the moment was not an affectation, the result of obstinacy or pedantry. It was not anything that had been preconceived, calculated, or planned over a long period. It sprang altogether naturally from a certain way of feeling and looking at things, which was supplemented by a need to vary the painter's artistic creations and to build up a stockpile of experiences. It was purely instinctive and spontaneous. Consequently, it was completely sincere even in its most troublesome aspects.

And when, suddenly, Ensor keeps repeating himself, at least he remains faithful to himself and does not seek to imitate anyone else, which for an artist is a form of honesty.

A «TALL SPLENETIC PIERROT»

«I was born,» James Ensor recounted, «on April 13, 1860, on a Friday, the day of Venus. Well! ... At my birth Venus came toward me, smiling, and we looked long into each other's eyes. Ah, what beautiful sea-green, blue-green eyes; what fine long hair, the color of sand. Venus was blonde and beautiful, all covered with foam. She smelt pleasantly of salt water.»

Throughout his life Ensor would be lulled by the murmur of waves on the shore. If until his dying day he remained faithful to Ostend, his native town, it was above all because of his love of the sea, that North Sea the «color of an oyster,» «insatiable drinker of bloody suns,» from which, one summer night, there arose «a fantastic black bird» that came swooping down through the window of his child's bedroom, shining like a beacon. (1)

In 1860, Ostend had a population of barely sixteen thousand people. However, it already responded to two different drumbeats. During ten months of the year, encircled by its turfy ramparts, with its fishermen's port smelling of tar and fresh fish, its dock where sailing ships were moored that evoked dreams of distant ports of call, its low houses whipped by the wind from the open sea, it was simply a small town, peaceful and a bit dismal. In July and August it became a fashionable seaside resort and was aroused from its torpor by the crowds of timid bathers and summer visitors seeking sea air. Gentlemen with beards like those of fauns, conventionally dressed and retaining a sober mien in any and all circumstances, languishing ladies dressed in crinolines and never seen without their parasols, and children with long curls, too well-behaved for their age, animated the beach, the dike, and the breakwater.

James Ensor's parents lived on the profits made during the tourist season. He was a «solid Englishman» and she a Flemish woman of old stock, «with a touch of Spanish blood»; they managed a shop at 44 rue Longue where they sold «souvenirs of Ostend»: shells, trinkets, curios, imported articles, and beach toys. At carnival time their stock was supplemented by «papier mâché» masks, fiery red, grotesque, and hilarious. A strange and colorful hodgepodge of objects! But the magic spell of a ray of sun or the gleam of a lamp were enough to give this miscellany of gimcracks an unexpected radiance and to create an unreal universe, as beautiful as a dream, a world of fantasy to fire the imagination of the young James. The fairyland of this enchanted shop was to be one of the principal sources of the painter's inspiration, the origin of the cosmic extravaganza produced by his unbridled and madly active imagination.

James was brought up in French, in a French-speaking milieu. It was only at the age of thirteen that he started school, at the Collège Notre-Dame. He detested school, just as he detested every sort of discipline. Yet he did not rebel openly. He was satisfied to appear indifferent, restive, and so resistant to learning as to discourage the most patient of teachers. After two unproductive years his parents were obliged to remove him from school.

---

(1) The quotations, for which there is no attribution, are excerpts from the «Writings of James Ensor.» They include articles which review art and artists, as well as some speeches and biographical data.

His mother indulged his whims. His father, « a superior sort of man » whose own ambitions had been thwarted, felt ill at ease in the limited existence to which he had been reduced and, reacting against bourgeois conventionality, he favored imaginative and creative ways. Both of them left James free to wander, to dream, to amble along the dunes and in the old port, to listen to the stories of ogres and the fairy tales dinned by an old Flemish maid and to take refuge in an attic « full of horrible spiders » in which were piled — familiar and marvelous sight — the reserve supplies for the family shop.

A new hobby of the lad of fifteen, who had been raised so haphazardly, revealed a talent which amazed his acquaintances: he drew or painted with watercolors everything which met his gaze. His father, convinced of his son's bent, had him given lessons by two obscure local water-colorists of whom the painter would say, « They initiated me professorially into the fallacious banalities of their dreary, narrow-minded and stillborn craft. »

Ensor's first trial efforts date from this period. They are hasty sketches, laborious and uncertain, but with the charm of freshness and a certain ingenuity. They are views of the environs of Ostend, painted in the open air, and they show an accurate vision and a keen perception of shadings: the flat Flemish countryside punctuated in red by the tile roofs of a few farmhouses scattered amid the greenery, the soft and tawny dunes with the sea breezes ruffling the clumps of marram grass, the bare and dreary beaches on which waves crested with foam break and then die. Already revealed, in what Ensor would later describe as « unpretentious little works painted in oil on pink cardboard, » is the influence exerted on the painter by the sea, his « great source of inspiration. » The gray and sea-green nuances of color in the waves are reflected in the sky. In the seascapes more than in any of his other pictures, the sky occupies an immense, overwhelming space. It is this same dense, opaque light which can be found in the most striking works marking the beginning of Ensor's career. « A secret instinct guided me, » he wrote, « an intuitive understanding of the maritime air, which I could sniff in the breeze, inhale in the pearly mist, draw from the briny waves and hear in the wind. »

When he was seventeen Ensor enrolled at the Académie des Beaux-Arts in Brussels. From the very first day « a serious misunderstanding developed. » They imposed on the youth, who had a feeling for color and for movement, the chore of drawing « all'antiqua » (from antique models). Nothing could have been more unacceptable to one of his temperament than such stiff academicism. Chilled by the atmosphere of the Academy, feeling chained and shackled, he began working « without enthusiasm »; then, very quickly, he decided to pay no more attention to their rules. The bold manner in which he copied the plaster models outraged his professors, the painters Joseph Stalleart, Jef Van Severdonck, and Alexandre Robert. Disconcerted by his unusual propensities and his individualistic experiments, they saw them as merely « ignorant pipe dreams. » However, they did not pressure him, allowed him to work as he would. This meant that he worked nonstop, like a fiend, determined to acquire all the technical pictorial skills that he needed. Nights, he « composed or geographized his dreams. »

At nineteen years of age, he made a firts attempt that was a masterstroke! Ensor painted the *Woman with Turned-Up Nose* (1879) (see p. 9), the portrait of a lowly servant who lacked beauty. « To prove to the painters of pretty women, » he wrote, « that a portrait has a right to be ugly. » This work was the real starting point of his « dark period. » The light was filtered and subdued. Its spirit and its heavy touch were the marks of a Flemish artist in love with truth. The work aimed to be realistic, but still revealed the influence of the Impressionists. « It has felt the grip of Manet, the caress of Renoir, » observed Paul Fierens.

In that same year Ensor produced three versions of a self-portrait, which were already permeated by a completely authentic Ensorian touch. The two first ones appear to be preliminary attempts leading up to the extraordinarily successful third version, *Artist at his Easel* (1879). The artist's conscious effort to show only what is essential and to stress the play of light makes this self-portrait at once a work of great psychological insight and of untrammeled esthetic boldness.

The following year Ensor left the Academy, which he called an « establishment for the short-sighted. » During the three years he spent studying there, he only won second prize for

The Cathedral, 1886   Etching, 9¼" × 7" (23,6 × 17,7 cm.)
Art Institute of Chicago. Joseph R. Shapiro Collection

Dangerous Cooks, 1896   Colored chalk, 9½" × 13" (24 × 33 cm.)   Museum Plantin-Moretus, Antwerp

drawing. This did not mean, however, that he did not knuckle down and work with a view to doing well in the competition for composition. To this end he painted several pictures of conventional subjects, the sort that was considered acceptable when academic awards were given. Among these was a canvas with a whimsical title, *Monks in a State of Exaltation Claiming the Body of the Theologian Oris in Spite of the Opposition of the Bishop of Friton or Friston.* The composition caused a great uproar. It so intrigued the director of the Academy, Jean Portaels, that for a long time he kept it in his office on display as a curiosity.

Although Ensor was undoubtedly a black sheep, his talents in drawing were so obvious that it was impossible to refuse to award him a prize. A whole series of large charcoal sketches devoted to «Ostend types» date from this apprenticeship period. *A Coal-man, The Boy, The Washerwoman, Fisherman with a Basket, Young Sailor,* are solidly constructed, using wide strokes and large masses to delineate bulk and volume. In an effort to achieve a synthesis, details are sacrificed to the effect as a whole. One might even say that these dark figures foretell those of Constant Permeke. In addition to this Ensor produced a multiplicity of rough drafts, characteristic drawings, and spontaneous renderings. He was constantly scribbling sketches in his notebook or on the first scrap of paper that came to hand — something he would continue to do throughout

WOMAN EATING OYSTERS, 1882   Oil on canvas, 81$\frac{1}{2}$″ × 59$\frac{1}{16}$″ (207 × 150 cm.)
Koninklijk Museum voor Schone Kunsten, Antwerp

his life. Taking note of this, poet Emile Verhaeren observed, « I take a certain paradoxical pleasure in stating that it is precisely the individual among our great artists who has been accused of being perhaps the one the least mindful of line drawing who in fact has cultivated it the most. »

At the age of twenty Ensor was a lanky young man, so thin and so pale that in Ostend they gave him the nickname of « Mr. Death's-Head. » Naturalistic novelist Camille Lemonnier spoke of his having the bearing of « a tall and splenetic Pierrot passing through life as if the eternal prey of hallucinations. » This extraordinary youth wore his hair « like an artist, » long and fluffy. His light eyes in turn gleamed with mischievousness and were misted over by dreams. His receding chin, indicating a less than strong will, was soon hidden under a short beard.

Sensitive, shy, even fearful, Ensor spoke little and appeared to be constantly on the defensive. An enemy of routine and conventional practices, wild and imaginative, passionate and skeptical, undisciplined and independent, curious and prying, rebellious and derisive, tender and candid, blunt and irreverent, touchy and easily hurt, he detested stupidity and could not stomach injustice. He was subject to fits of indignation and anger. He was very much aware of the sap which seethed within him. He was utterly sincere, believed completely in what he was doing, proved to be both patient and stubborn, and refused to make concessions.

FROM NATURALISM TO IMPRESSIONISM

In 1880 Ostend with its new and shining villas, its big hotels, and its horrible « Kursaal » (Casino), began to gain a reputation as the « queen of seaside resorts. » The Ensors moved their shop to the ground floor of a large building that had been constructed shortly before and that was at the corner of the Rue de Flandre and the Boulevard Van-Iseghem. They saw their grown son return to the fold with the intention of settling down there. The young man took possession of an attic and although it was illuminated only by a faint light that came in through the single window and a skylight, he managed to set it up as a studio. James Ensor had made a decision. Without meaning any disrespect to the gentlemen of the Academy, he would henceforth devote himself to painting.

From his high perch under the eaves his gaze descended to the Rue de Flandre, which he was to paint so often, then rested on the rooftops, another subject which was to frequently intrigue him and, in the distance, looked beyond at the far countryside. If he leaned out of the window he could perceive the sea close by, the sea whose muted murmur filled all of the attic studio. Between the four walls of this aerie one canvas succeeded another under the impetus of the painter's brush. All were vigorous, original, and bold. There were at least thirty the first year! Between 1880 and 1900, from the time he was twenty until he was forty, Ensor was to produce his best and most characteristic pictures. It was, indeed, the era of his masterpieces.

At the beginning, influenced by Naturalism, he chose his subjects from daily life and even, occasionally, from the most insignificant aspects of that daily life.

Ensor discovered his typical natives of Ostend by chance in the course of his wanderings — nose to the wind, eyes ever alert, pencil in hand — in the old quarters of the city, stinking of fish and poverty, and in the alleys bordered by low houses in which plaice and dabs were drying in the windows. He depicted either these popular types, that he saw around him, or else painted genre scenes in which he recreated the intimate atmosphere of bourgeois interiors, or portraits for which he had the people around him pose, or self-portraits filled with perceptive psychological insight. Looking at the dates of these works, one can already observe how many and how varied were the genres at which he was trying his hand, and to what extent they were combined and interwoven.

A digression is in order. It is essential that one not try to see in Ensor anything other than what he was, that is to say a pure artist. Whatever may have been said and repeated by overly zealous and well-intentioned writers, the common people did not interest him as members of a social class. He did not waste any pity on these miserable, unfortunate wretches. Their lot was certainly a sad one, but was not life itself sad, for the privileged as well as for the lowly? In

Portrait of Ernest Rousseau, 1887   Drypoint, 9″ × 6⁵⁄₈″ (22,8 × 16,8 cm.)
Collection: Mr. and Mrs. Herman D. Shickman

24   WOMAN IN DISTRESS, 1882   Oil on canvas, 39³⁄₈″ × 31¹⁄₂″ (100 × 80 cm.)
Musée national d'Art moderne, Paris

Ensor's opinion, it was an absurd comedy at which he felt compelled to laugh and which, as far as he was concerned, was nothing more than a game. The problems of the world in which he lived were not his concern as long as they did not involve a threat to artistic beauty. He was a painter. His sole concern was art, an art which he did not feel compelled to use to plead the cause of the masses. He had none of the hallmarks of what today might be called a politically committed artist. When, in the course of his painting, he chanced to castigate the evils of the social system or deplore the injustices of life, he did so not as a moralist or a sociologist but as a creative artist eager to employ any available materials in his work and to take advantage of any known data. He was not an advocate for any person or for any philosophy. As a matter of fact, for this individualist without illusions the only subject matter worthy of attention was the individual who — like all the rest of us, actually — alone and solitary, walked through life to his inexorable fate. Indeed, he could be heard more frequently raising his voice on behalf of animals who were victims of vivisection than on behalf of his peers. Likewise, popular subjects attracted him only because they were often picturesque and colorful. He turned to them solely because he found in them appealing subjects to paint.

His portraits of Ostend types were an extension and further development of the charcoal studies which had permitted him to try his hand at shaping forms and contours. Their value lies in this rather than in their coloring, which consisted of neutral and cloudy shades, highlighted soberly. They are sketched with large strokes, an expansive touch, clean lines, and great areas of shading. Here again the painter restricted himself to what was basic and ignored any frills. Yet his people are none the less brought to life with their social significance and their psychological identities intact, thanks to what he suggests even more than what he depicts outright.

The most remarkable picture in *The Lamp Boy* (1880) (see p. 10). The youth is wearing dark clothes and is silhouetted against a solid background, a little chap sturdily planted on strong legs with large feet. In his hands is a brass lamp that sends out flashes of light which instantly attract the attention of the viewer, beginning with the boy. His head is bent forward. His eyes are hidden by the visor of his cap. One can see only the bottom part of his face. Yet how telling is his expression! How powerfully evocative! This ship's boy or apprentice represents all of the lads of the underprivileged class who are forced to work at too young an age, who are malnourished, and who lead a joyless and hopeless existence. Was Ensor thinking of all this when he painted him? Surely not. He was simply concerned with seeking out truth. He found it and painted what he found, nothing more. But it was indeed a great deal.

The Lamp Boy is indisputably the best work of his popular series, in spite of the lively realism of *Sick Tramp Warming Himself* (1882), a canvas destroyed in the bombardment of Ostend in May 1940; in spite of the impact, as brutal as a knockout blow, of *The Drunkards* (1883) (see p. 30), two characters in distress, deplorable and disturbing, tragic in their drunkenness; in spite of the bravura piece entitled *The Rower* (1883) (see p. 31), a composition which happens to be more conventional and slightly stereotyped, with exaggerations and distortions that foreshadow the techniques of Expressionism.

Drawing its inspiration from the same source was a work which appeared much later, *Melancholy Fishwives* (1892), two bonneted and gossipy old crones such as could be seen in fish markets. Their gaze vague and unfocused while three skeletons, whose heads emerge from a mirror, seem to be eargely waiting for their imminent victims, they are expressive of a confusion and disarray which excited the imagination of the painter. The composition is sharp, caustic, almost a caricature. «Death unto them! They have eaten too much fish,» reads a sign brandished by the skeletons. The two miserable existences which are coming to an end without finding anything substantial to hang onto are truly sad. Yet in spite of everything Ensor, who refused to acknowledge either sentimentality or pomposity, could see the funny side of the situation.

Ensor's interior scenes, his figures, and his portraits all reflect a common style. The importance given to the ambience in the figure compositions renders them comparable to the interior scenes. And the figures are also portraits, as are the persons painted in some of the interior scenes. There is a unity in diversity which is typical of Ensor.

The interior scenes are based on incidents in provincial bourgeois society at the time of Ensor's youth. Life in those days was self-contained, peaceful, confined within narrow perimeters, secure and fairly monotonous, as is apparent at once from the various decors: parlors which look as if they smell musty, with drawn curtains and slipcovers on the chairs. There is not very much light and particularly no sunlight! In his parent's home, Ensor had lived in just such surroundings. But since he was Flemish, he did not find it enough to enjoy the confined existence of a recluse. He needed air and light. And he put them in his paintings.

What novelist Eugène Demolder, his friend, wrote concerning *Somber Lady* (1881) (see p. 11) could apply equally well to Ensor's other canvases, «What a golden song, powerful and resonant, is sung by the light penetrating the lowered great yellow shade, coming through the curtains onto the plush and the slipcovers! One can sense the presence of the sky and the sun behind the closed and peaceful window, and the recitation of the beautiful poem of warm light somehow makes it seem one is breathlessly waiting for the visit of a woman of captivating prettiness!»

These sifted sunbeams and the play of light which caresses the objects it touches accentuates the intimacy of the interior. At the same time they outline and illuminate persons as well as things, they bring about a fusion of people and their milieu, a oneness which is definitely Impressionistic. The models acquire a kind of personality which would not have been possible in a monochrome treatment. Each scene, without a dramatic statement and limited to a simple notation of fact, thus gains in intensity and profits from an especially deep significance. Paul Fierens wrote, «*Afternoon at Ostend* (1881) (see p. 13) and the *Bourgeois Salon* (1881), which might have been merely satirical descriptions, become, thanks to a strongly executed lighting effect, marvelous poems, domestic symphonies.»

Consider also *The Colorist* (1880), the first work to be exhibited by the Ostend painter, the following year, at the «Cercle de la Chrysalide» (Chrysalis) in Brussels, *Woman with a Fan* (1880), *Woman in Blue* (1881), *Woman in Distress* (1882) (see p. 24), *Woman with a Red Umbrella* (1885), and *Children Dressing* (1886). In them Ensor's art is restrained and discreet, its realism tempered by a spiritual quality. It is an art which is evocative rather than descriptive. The same is true of *Russian Music* (1881) (see p. 16). «There is no emphasis on unrestrained violence,» stressed the poet Emile Verhaeren in analyzing it, «but a series of nuances and subdued touches, as if a frail, strange, soft music, which one is supposed to listen to, somehow dominates the painting.»

As for *Woman Eating Oysters* (1882) (see p. 21), a composition which in its perspective, the proportions of the subject and, above all, the lightness of its colors, explores new frontiers, Verhaeren saw in it «the first truly bright canvas produced on our shores,» by which he meant Belgium. It took nothing more than that to cause it to be rejected by the Antwerp Salon. The explanation offered the painter, «There will be some much worse pictures in the Salon, but we cannot encourage such tendencies.»

That says it all. The tendencies displayed by Ensor were new and revolutionary. Up to that time, light had been considered as merely complementary to the technical development of a picture. It had never occupied the center of the stage, so to speak. It had never been employed as a separate and distinct part of the whole, with its own life and identity. The important contribution made by Ensor was that in this respect he was responsible for a revolution that accounts in large part for the nature of contempory art.

Incidentally, it was not so much light in and of itself which shocked the organizers of the Salons in Antwerp and elsewhere as it was the technique that painting it required on the part of the artist. «Light devours objects,» Ensor would observe. At the very least it erodes the outlines of objects while highlighting their surfaces. What the established order could not bring itself to accept was precisely this nibbling at the outlines of objects so that they became vague and blurred.

James Ensor's problem was that he was born too soon. He anticipated «in every sense,» as he would say — by a quarter of a century the experimentation of modern painters. He struck out against conformity and smug placidity. He upset ingrained habits and conventional attitudes. This was why his contemporaries could not forgive him. «A too young revolutionary,» wrote

Grand View of Mariakerke, 1887 Etching, 8¼" × 10¼" (20,8 × 25,9 cm.)
Art Institute of Chicago. Print and Drawing Fund

Firmin Cuypers, «out of place in the period during which he emerged, Ensor was not made welcome or well received, and people refused to acknowledge that his painting offered the still partially unrevealed spirit of a new age which had just been born with him.»

There are few large portraits in Ensor's work, and those which exist date from his dark period. Here again are evidences of a new technique. Outlines tend to fade away and forms are drowned under creamy, sometimes juicy coats of thick paint, which present contrasts of light and shade. But this is more than a simple emphasis on contrasts. It is really a confrontation, especially in the *Portrait of Willy Finch* (c. 1882) (see p. 32). «This portrait,» wrote Paul Haesaerts, «is one of those painted by Ensor which, on the surface of a human face, best depicts the meeting of light and shadow, their harmony and their disagreements, their struggle and their mutual accommodations.»

Angry Masks, 1883
Charcoal, 29½" × 23⅝"
(75 × 60 cm.)
Collection:
Marcel Mabille, Brussels

Portrait of the Artist's Father (1881) (see p. 14) is constructed with a base of geometric planes and painted with a palette knife. He used a thick paste, which looks as if it had been shoveled on with a trowel, to produce flashing streaks of blue and white. The color which the artist seemed to prefer at that stage dominates *Woman with Blue Shawl* (1882), the image of a generation that was on the verge of disappearing. Contrasting with the coloring of these two canvases is *Portrait of the Artist's Mother* (1881) (see p. 15). This is a symphony in brown, russet, sepia, and beige, over which, like a pleasantly discordant note, is the startling splash of three roses fastened to the opening at the woman's throat: one crimson, another yellow, the third white.

In each instance the faces are clear and plainly drawn, even though the touch is light and spontaneous. The individual personality comes through unmistakably. In the eyes, the expressions, the wrinkles on the foreheads, the shapes of the noses, and the lines of the mouths can be discerned the characteristic traits of the particular subjects. One can rediscover in these impressions what is already known of their pasts. The fleshy face of Ensor's father has features which indicate his lack of assurance, the disillusion caused by a destiny which has not measured

ANGRY MASKS, 1883   Oil on canvas, 53⅜″ × 44⅛″ (135 × 112 cm.)
Musées Royaux des Beaux-Arts de Belgique, Brussels

29

THE DRUNKARDS, 1883   Oil on canvas, 45¹/₄″ × 64¹⁵/₁₆″ (115 × 165 cm.)
Collection: Georges de Graeve, Brussels

30

THE ROWER, 1883   Oil on canvas, 31⅛″ × 39″ (79 × 99 cm.)
Koninklijk Museum voor Schone Kunsten, Antwerp

PORTRAIT OF WILLY FINCH, c. 1882   Oil on canvas, 19½″ × 11⅝″ (49,5 × 29,5 cm.)
Stedelijk Museum, Ostend

up to his ambitions and which he has not been able to control. The thin and angular visage of Ensor's mother reveals that she was an energetic, cautious woman, blessed with a plentiful supply of common sense, and possibly ruled by her head rather than by her heart.

As a matter of fact, the features that the painter depicts the most frequently are his own. He lends them to various characters in his work, including the image of Christ, who sometimes ressembles him so closely he might be his brother. He also does himself the honor of using himself as a model in several of his paintings. Among the self-portraits which he executed during this period, it is essential to take note of the admirable *Self-Portrait in a Flowered Hat* (1883) (see title page) that marks a decisive turning point in what, with his love of puns, he amusingly called « the art of Ensor » (« art Ensor » which sounds like « hareng saur », red herring). This work brings to mind the work of Rubens. Ensor portrayed himself in the same manner as the Antwerp master had depicted himself two centuries earlier. He wore a hat in imitation of his illustrious model, but made it a fantastically fancy headpiece. Then he went still further and produced an irreverent parody by painting himself à la Rubens in carnival attire with a plumed headdress, comical, absurd, and ridiculous, in *Portrait of Ensor with Masks* (1899). In this picture he is surrounded, encircled, squeezed between figures with grimacing « papier-mâché » faces.

Let us make no mistake. These extraordinary compositions, which at first glance make one smile, are far from being mere jokes. In *Self-Portrait in a Flowered Hat* the expression in the eyes is anxious and almost sad. The expression of the subject and the fantasy of the accessories are in sharp contrast. The pleasure found in contemplating the latter is very quickly tempered by a certain reservation, because the drollery of the image is offset by something profoundly bitter, the expression of a soul in torment. As to the frozen faces of *Portrait of Ensor with Masks*, the distorted and bloated visages, like those of gargoyles on cathedrals, what do they represent if not human emotions?

People have striven hard to recognize Rubens' influence and that of various other painters on Ensor's work. Names mentioned beside Rubens include Rembrandt, Jordaens, Snyders, Goya, Turner, Rowlandson and also, with greater justification, the names of Bruegel the Elder and Bosch. True, Emile Verhaeren, his friend, has testified that Ensor admired Rembrandt, as well as Chardin, Watteau, Ingres, and Delacroix. But can one really say that he borrowed from his predecessors their ways of seeing things and expressing them in artistic terms? At the very most in can be stated that he revealed an affinity for some among them. But one must look elsewhere for the wellsprings of Ensor's torrential talent.

They are to be found in the painter's roots: the Flemish earth; the scenery and ambience of Ostend; the proximity of the sea, a haunting and bewitching presence; the Belgian sky, with its own unique light. And then there are the works which he read. Ensor, a self-educated man, must have read a great deal to become what he was. We know that he read time and time again Balzac and Poe, that he was fond of Rabelais and Cervantes' Don Quixote, a character destined to appeal to him.

Moreover, he must have been influenced by the artistic currents that had been making themselves felt ever since, at an early age, he had dedicated himself to art.

The beginning of Ensor's career in 1880 coincided with the heroic period of Impressionism. The Impressionist painters, with Manet, Monet, Pissarro, Degas, Sisley, Cézanne and Renoir at the head of the movement, were still struggling for acceptance. Six years after their first exhibition they were barely beginning to be appreciated by a very small segment of the public. Their financial situation was still precarious. The establishment was hostile to them. The doors of the Salons remained closed to them. But their esthetic ideas were starting to circulate. They had made some progress. Someting new was on the march. And Ensor, looking to the future, showed himself to be considerably more receptive to the contemporary trends that they espoused than to the ideas of the past.

Yet one would misunderstand and underestimate him if one believed that he accepted the views of others without examining them, weighing them, studying them from every angle, and finally modifying them so that they were consistent with his personality and adapted to his

GIRL WITH DOLL, 1884
Oil on canvas,
58⅞″ × 35⅞″
(149 × 91 cm.)
Wallraf Richartz Museum,
Cologne
◁

▷
VASE OF FLOWERS, 1883
Oiltype on fabric,
44½″ × 38⅜″
(113 × 97,5 cm.)
The Minneapolis
Institute of Arts.
Gift in memory
of Mrs. Conrad Driscoll

34

particular temperament. His Impressionism is different from French Impressionism in that it is more sober, more restrained, and reflects the dreamy, moody quality of the Flemish soul. Also, it is the result of a much more stubborn determination to develop and grow. As far as Ensor, a relentless advocate of experimentation, was concerned, the French Impressionists did not go far enough in the area of research and testing. He described them — and this may prove shocking to the reader — as «superficial wielders of the brush, mired in the mud of traditional formulas.» What distinguished him from them was the fact that he was more interested than they in the subtleties of light and contrasts of color.

«Ensor's Impressionism,» declared Paul Fierens, «blossoms in a vision in which at first sensuality has the upper hand, and in which afterward the mind and emotions give life to the canvas and animate the drawing, the outlines, the strokes.» He added, «Ensor has moved beyond Impressionism, gracefully soaring above it and elegantly thumbing his nose at is.»

ESCAPE TO THE LIGHT

After what is known as his «dark period» — although the darkness was relative and the term was justified only if the darkness was contrasted with the luminosity of his «bright period,» — in 1883 there began for Ensor what Paul Fierens described as a «climb to the light,» a period during which the artist's palette can be seen to grow lighter and his canvases to be illuminated by warm and vibrant tones. Of all the phases in Ensor's evolution, this is the one which can be explained the most easily. The sky in Ostend, like the sky throughout Flanders, throughout all of the north country, for most of the year is misty, gray, and hangs low over the land. One might long to see clouds forming moving shapes, thus animating the heavens and revealing between them patches of blue through which light could fall on the earth below. Alas! There is nothing but a veritable dark awning which stretches from one horizon to the other. It is a cheerless sky, which extinguishes the light, blots out colors, and creates in those under its spell a mood of depression and melancholy. This is the sky under which Ensor lived, the sky whose hazy luminescence only too often bathed the subjects he painted.

This environmental factor was a major influence in the early period of his work. At first constrained by the discipline of Verism and Naturalism, he reproduced things just as he saw them in a thin light. Using neutral tones for his palette — grays, browns, sepias, deep ochers — he had them play on his canvases only as filtered reflections. At this time he was twenty or just slightly older. But the farther along life's path an individual advances, the more he thirsts for paradise. On this earth paradise is youth, love, beauty, joy and also color, light, the caress and the sparkle of the sun. It was not long before the day came when Ensor experienced an increasing repugnance for the grayness which blurred all the objects around him, making them appear sad and dreary and casting a pall of gloom over his soul. In a reaction against this, he started to make his canvases sing by covering them with lively, luminous, glowing colors: yellows, reds, greens, colors to gladden the eye and the heart. Shortly afterward, lashing out against the wretchedness of human existence as he knew it, he disregarded wisdom and logic and plunged into poetic creations that were completely free of the dull weight of reason. The luminosity of his bright period is nothing other than a stubborn revolt against daily reality, an escape to the light. «We are hungry ("faim") for light,» he wrote, «and light is our guiding star ("fin").» (In French this remark of Ensor's is a pun as «faim» and «fin» are pronounced alike.) During his dark period, in which dark shades predominated, a diffuse light touched his work only furtively. On the contrary, light overwhelmed and literally bathed the canvases of the bright period. Straightforward, lively, and bountiful, it assumed a greater importance than the human figures and gave a soul and life to inanimate objects — «the mute neighbors in our lives,» as Ensor's friend Demolder called them. «In its pure state,» Ensor declared, «painting is the sun, the sky, the day, light, still more light and always light!» Henceforth that was to be his credo. Léo Van Puyvelde called him «a man obsessed by light.»

THE ROOFS OF OSTEND, 1885   Oil on canvas, 43″ × 52⅝″ (109,2 × 133,7 cm.)
Collection: Louis Franck, Esq., C.B.E. Gstaad

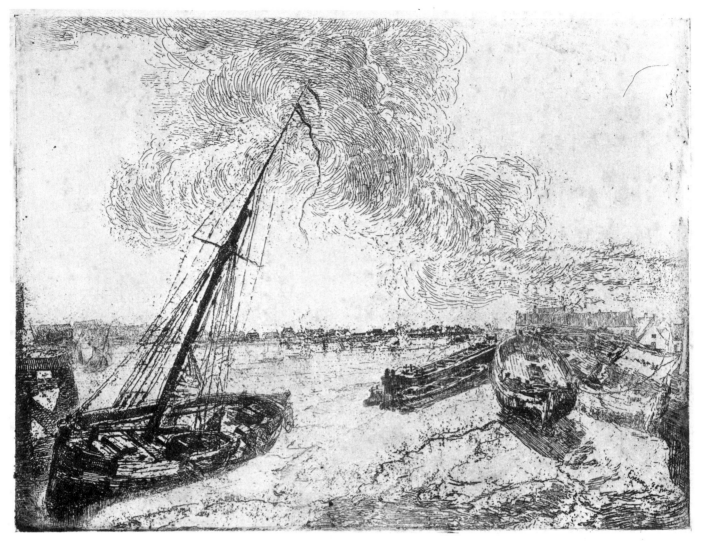

Boats Aground, 1888   Etching, 7" × 9⅜" (17,6 × 23,7 cm.)
Art Institute of Chicago. Print and Drawing Fund

He considered his concerns far removed from the experiments of the practitioners of Pointillism such as Seurat. «They are seeking only to reproduce the vibration of light,» he said disdainfully. And he judged them to be «already finished as far as light and art are concerned.» In his pictures, light corresponds to the definition which the painter Jacob Smits invented, «Light is matter.» All of Ensor's work is made up of this matter. To anyone who congratulated him on his choice of subjects, Ensor would reply without hesitation, «They are not subjects, they are lights.» His love of light, supplemented by his taste for experimentation, led him to produce a new bright version of *Afternoon at Ostend* (c. 1910). It was an interesting experiment, which resulted in a veritable re-creation in a different light. Forms which were originally shrouded in darkness this time were, as Paul Haesaerts said, «diluted by the light.»

With this advent of light came a corollary: the triumph of pure, bright color, without any factor which could diminish its brilliance and freshness. Henceforth Ensor's canvases would glory

Harbor of Ostend, 1888   Etching, 7¹/₁₆″ × 9³/₈″ (17,9 × 23,8 cm.)
Art Institute of Chicago. Print and Drawing Fund

in an outpouring of color, unequivocal, keen, and intense. He especially favored greens and reds, «two vital, splendid colors.» The painter advised that all of these colors had to be arranged «in such a way as to inspire discussion and foment ideas.» He added, «Colors which are badly distributed and coupled engage in a war to the death with one another and make terrible and hostile neighbors.»

Some of his canvases that are at the edge of realistic figuration, such as *Tribulations of Saint Anthony* (1887) (see p. 40), *Christ in Agony* (1888) (see p. 52), and *The Rebel Angels Struck Down* (1889) (see p. 53), are nothing more than trickles of color mixed with torrents of light. «Everything is constructed by the paintbrush, but everything endures only through color,» Firmin Cuypers remarked admiringly. «That is the miracle!»

Ensor, «a visionary avid of color,» celebrated it lyrically. «Color, the vital center for the masters of our region. Color of the infinite seas, color of the salt meadows where curly sheep

TRIBULATIONS OF ST. ANTHONY, 1887 Oil on canvas, 46⅜″ × 66″ (117,8 × 167,6 cm.)
The Museum of Modern Art, New York

40

tenderly graze on sugar-sweet buds ... Color, the adornment of the sea, of mermaids, and of women, joy of our eyes, giving enchantment to painting ... Let us heighten all our colors, so that they sing, so that they laugh, so that they shout their joy aloud!»

At the same time Ensor's realism was becoming increasingly spiritual, as if the painter had discovered the true value of people and things. What subject could more appropriately express his new attitude than the life of Christ? Scenes depicting its highlights abound in his work; examples of deviltry appear almost as frequently. This agnostic treated the life and the Passion of Jesus in a very personal manner, consciously placing them in an ambience which was either fantastic or supernaturel, in order to attest to their extraterrestrial nature. In *Christ in Agony,* a swarm of tiny creatures evokes the image of the humanity about to be redeemed; in *Christ Calming the Storm* (1891) (see pp. 68, 69) a gigantic whirlwind tosses and mingles clouds and waves.

Ensor gives everything a new significance, up to and including his landscapes and still lifes, which acquire an immaterial quality. He pursues the elusive, bringing underlying layers to the surface. Charles Sternberg expressed it well, «Penetrating his thick or thin coats of paint, as the case may be, one comes upon a core of phantasmagoria which endows nature with a disquieting appearance.» Nothing was better adapted to the touch of Ensor's brush than the reproduction of oceanic expanses; for nothing, in spite of its deceptive look of uniformity, is more changing than the sea. «Three hundred and sixty-five thousand times a year, when the moon laughs or a cloud passes over it or sprinkles moisture, it changes its dress, its shirt and its mood.»

However, more is the pity that this painter who was so much in love with the sea has left us only a few pictures that reproduce it directly. In his all too rare seascapes he strove to show the subtle relationship that exists between sky and water. Each of these canvases is a harmony of light and color, animated by the moving play of shadows, the undulating shapes of clouds, the ceaseless motion of waves. Ensor's paintings pay homage to the sea just as his prose is a verbal tribute to it. «My beloved sea, I should like to celebrate with a fresh bouquet, without surrealist pretensions, your hundred faces, your surface, your multifaceted planes and your dimpled splendor, your ruby-red deeps, your diamond-studded crests, your sapphire peaks, your blessings, your delights, your unparalleled charms.»

What did he not owe to the sea, «the pure sea, which awakes our energies and claims our unfailing constancy!» Very simply he owed to it the fact that he was what he was. «It is the ocean,» said Jozef Muls, «it is the North Sea which shaped Ensor's soul. His lungs are filled with the breath of the open sea, his eyes have measured its infinite expanses. It is the sea which gives such unusual brightness to his canvases.»

It is interesting to note that, apart from his tributes to the sea there are relatively few landscapes, in the usual sense of the word, in his painted work — *Tower of Lisseweghe* (1888) (see p. 56) is an example of one. It is rather in his engravings that we find them, and these examples are numerous. He preferred to use a paintbrush for his urban scenes — the different versions of *Vlaanderenstraat* (1880 [see p. 12], 1881, 1891) and of *Roofs of Ostend* (1885 [see p. 37], 1898, 1906) — as well as a few pictures in which the sea plays some part — *Carnival on the Beach* (1887), *The Sloops* (1890) (see p. 42), *Boats Aground* (c. 1892) (see p. 38), and *The Canal* (1902).

Above all, it is in his still lifes that Ensor reveals himself to be a virtuoso in the treatment of color. The paintings of his dark period, such as the admirable *Still Life with Blue Pitcher* (1890–91) (see p. 66) and the first version of *Still Life with Ray* (1882), are developed with muted tones. In the pictures which followed, the light is of such radiant brilliance that there is no place for shade or shadow. Relief is expressed solely through gradations of color and reflections, through the relationship between brightness and shade — *Still Life with Ray* (1892) (see p. 67), *Still Life with Kale* (1892), and *Still Life with Shells* (1895) (see back cover). In some instances the outlines have even disappeared, melted, devoured by the light, and shapes take form only because of the coloring — *Still Life with Fruits* (1889).

It is in his still lifes that, to cite the words of Paul Haesaerts, one sees the painter «try to find a solution to the expression of form through the use of color.»

COUNTRY FAIR NEAR
A WINDMILL, 1889
Etching, hand colored,
5⅜″ × 6⅞″
(13,8 × 17,8 cm.)
Gallery Le Bateau-Lavoir
Paris

THE SLOOPS
(THE FISHING DOCKS
IN OSTEND), 1888
Etching, hand colored,
6⅞″ × 9¼″
(17,7 × 23,5 cm.)
Gallery Le Bateau-Lavoir,
Paris

FIGHT OF THE DEMONS (DEVILS THRASHING ANGELS AND ARCHANGELS), 1888
Etching, hand colored, 10¼″ × 12⅜″ (26 × 31,4 cm.) Gallery Le Bateau-Lavoir, Paris

EXPRESSIONISM AND PHANTASMAGORIA

At the very moment when the path ahead seemed clear, Ensor did an unexpected about-face and revealed himself as a potential rival of a Jerome Bosch or a Pieter Bruegel: He abandoned Realism and Impressionism for Expressionism and Surrealism as a result of a surprisingly rapid metamorphosis which defied all logic.

In 1883 an unexpected element entered into his work and gave him an entirely new orientation: masks. These masks in «papier-mâché,» ruddy or pale, hilarious, dazed or mischievous were the grotesque carnival accessories at which he had gazed so raptly in the wonderful shop of dreams he had known in childhood and which he encountered with every step he took in the streets of Ostend during carnival revelries. He made them one of his favorite motifs. Instead of limiting himself to reproducing them in his still lifes, as in *Attributes of the Studio* (1889) (see p. 51), he uses them to adorn the characters brought to life by his brush. Despite the apparent buffoonery something troubling and ferocious cuts through the drollery of these bloated and grimacing masks that are so effectively concealing faces and personalities. Are we looking at humanity, disguised and cryptic, hovering on the border between dream and reality, or are we

The Assassination, 1888   Etching, 6¹⁵/₁₆″ × 9⁵/₁₆″ (17,8 × 23,8 cm.)
Yale University Art Gallery, Gift of James N. Elesh

The Entry of Christ into Brussels, 1888 (detail)

THE ENTRY OF CHRIST INTO BRUSSELS, 1888   Oil on canvas, 101⅜″ × 149¼″ (256,8 × 378,4 cm.)
Collection: Louis Franck, Esq., C.B.E. Gstaad

THE ENTRY OF CHRIST INTO BRUSSELS, 1888 (details)

THE ENTRY OF CHRIST INTO BRUSSELS, 1888 (detail)

50

ATTRIBUTES OF THE STUDIO, 1889   Oil on canvas, 35⅝″ × 44½″ (83 × 113 cm.)
Bayerische Staatsgemäldesammlungen, Munich

CHRIST IN AGONY, 1888   Oil on canvas, 6¼″ × 8¼″ (16 × 21 cm.)
Collection: Marcel Mabille, Brussels

THE REBEL ANGELS STRUCK DOWN, 1888   Oil on canvas, 43⁵/₁₆″ × 52³/₄″ (110 × 134 cm.)
Koninklijk Museum voor Schone Kunsten, Antwerp

THE ASTONISHMENT OF THE MASK WOUZE, 1889
Oil on canvas, 42$^{15}/_{16}$" × 52" (109 × 132 cm.)
Koninklijk Museum voor Schone Kunsten, Antwerp

▷

PORTRAIT OF OLD WOMAN WITH MASKS, 1889
Oil on canvas, 21$^{1}/_{4}$" × 18$^{3}/_{4}$" (54 × 47,5 cm.)
Museum voor Schone Kunsten, Ghent

Tower of Lisseweghe, 1888
Oil on canvas, 24″ × 28¾″ (61 × 73 cm.)
Collection: Louis Franck, Esq., C.B.E. Gstaad

▷

The Multiplication of the Fishes, 1891
Etching on copper, printed in black, 7″ × 9⅜″ (18 × 23,8 cm.)
Art Institute of Chicago. Gift of the Print and Drawing Club

really seeing a parade of masquerading specters in *Angry Masks* (1883) (see p. 29), *The Stranger* (1888), *Masks Confronting Death* (1888), *The Astonishment of the Mask Wouze* (1889) (see p. 54), *Portrait of Old Woman with Masks* (1889) (see p. 55), *The Intrigue* (1890) (see front cover and pp. 62–63), *Masks Fighting for the Body of a Hanged Man* (1891) (see p. 65), *The Assassination* (1891) (see etching, p. 44), *Strange Masks* (1891), *The Despair of Pierrot* (1892), and *Masks and Death* (1897) (see p. 84)?

Perhaps the skeletons, macabre and fantastic allegories which would soon be added to the list of the painter's favorite subjects are these same persons stripped bare: *Skeleton Studying Chinoiseries* (1885), *Skeletons Quarrelling over a Red Herring* (1891), *Pierrot and Skeleton in Yellow Robe* (1893), *Skeletons Warming Themselves* (1895) (see p. 85), *Skeletons in the Studio* (1900).

Why masks, and what power did the painter attribute to them? «Tracked down by my pursuers,» he commented, «I joyously took refuge in the solitary place where masks hold away, compounded of violence, light and brilliance. Masks mean to me freshness of color, shrillness of expression, sumptuous decoration, expansive unexpected gestures, uncoordinated movements.» The explanation is unsatisfactory and leaves the question unanswered.

Did Ensor wish to demonstrate that in his opinion life, however tragic it might be, was nothing more than a farce at which one might better laugh? Yet his laughter was through gritted

The Sad and Broken: Satan and His Fantastic Legions Tormenting the Crucified Christ, 1888
Pencil and charcoal, 24" × 29⅞" (61 × 76 cm.) Musées Royaux des Beaux-Arts de Belgique, Brussels

teeth, giving cause for thought. It is possible that obsessed by death — the other farce that is a fitting counterpart to the farce of life but even more somber and gloomy — he was seeking to evoke what lay beyond the grave in the form of strange and dehumanized shadows, often accompanied by telltale skeletons?

In order to rid himself of the hallucinations of a tormented and possibly morbid mind, did he transfer them to his canvases? Not Ensor, who was a sturdy fellow in robust health, mentally as well as physically. It is all too clear he was not duped by the fantastic universe that he created — an unreal world full of marvels, a world of dreams and nightmares — but rather that he was entertained and amused. Yet in his creations, gratuitous, comical, fantastic, and disconcerting as they appear underneath the buffoonery lies an air of tragedy. From them there emanates an impression of uneasiness, of anxiety. Anguish and humor coexist.

Could the painter have meant to evoke passion and vice, intermingled with some rare examples of virtue, by superimposing their caricatured images on unknown and unknowable faces? Under his brush, these masks come to life. They are the very faces of the people wearing them. In most of them the eyes can be seen. Oh, their gaze, sharp dull, threatening or sardonic, is terrible to contemplate, almost unendurable. Motionless, the masks wait. For what? We cannot know. That is what renders them so disturbing.

Perhaps all of this, in the long run, was simply a game, consistent with Ensor's taste for farce: He was a gentleman without an ounce of serious blood in his veins, whom yellowed photographs show extracting from his cranium the «madness stone,» gnawing at human bones swiped from a friend who was a medical student, and having fun by disguising himself and donning second hand clothes. We are told that he even played the flute through the nose.

What can we think, what can we say when, as Paul Fierens wrote, «dreams are married to reality and transform daily routines into something extraordinary»?

From a pictorial point of view, the colors in Ensor's masquerades are exceptionally opaque. Some canvases, such as *Portrait of Old Woman with Masks,* represent «a condensation of Ensor's art,» according to Paul Haesaerts. They bear witness to the creative powers of the painter. When one realizes that he started along this path in the same year he produced works such as *The Drunkards* and *The Rower,* one is amazed. What a powerful impact is exerted by these masks clothed in rags; they appear so contrary to expectations and reason that their incongruous image has remained more vivid in the public's memory than have any of the other pictures by this same artist!

Demons Teasing Me, 1888   Etching, 8⅝" × 11¾" (21,8 × 29,8 cm.)
Art Institute of Chicago. Joseph R. Shapiro Restricted Gift

«Art's precious song is sung endlessly and eternally ... Everything is fit stuff for the painter's brush, everything is good to paint, everything is beautiful to paint,» proclaimed Ensor, who worked frantically, undertaking all types of painting and all sorts of subjects, each time adapting his technique to the requirements of the moment, always making his robust and unique personality felt. The man of Ostend occasionally returned to the source of his inspiration. It amused him to paint, with satiric strokes, humorous cartoons and caricatures: *Ensor and General Léman Discuss Painting* (1890) (see p. 78), *The Good Judges* (1894) (see p. 71), *The Wicked Physicians* (1895) (see p. 70) and *Dangerous Cooks* (1896) (see p. 20). At times he was a religious painter in the style of the Pre-Raphaelites: *Consoling Virgin* (1892). He tried to emulate the gallantry school (a Watteau using mellow, blended, bright colors!): *The Garden of Love* (1898) (see pp. 73, 76). Above all, he liked to blaze new paths.

His most characteristic, most amaging, most stunning, most disconcerting, most controversial work bears the date of 1888: *The Entry of Christ into Brussels* (see pp. 45, 46–47, 48, 49, 50), a vast canvas more than thirty-six square feet (eleven meters). It is striking, bizarre, rowdy, loud, what Flaubert might have called «henormous,» and borders on the sacrilegious. In it we see a haloed Christ, making a gesture of blessing, mounted on an ass, and surrounded by obsequious masks. He advances in the middle of an indescribable cortege, which opens up and which, in the foreground, appears to walk out of the frame, amidst a swarming and gesticulating crowd; in a carnival atmosphere, with pennants and banners, there emerges a group of musicians playing a fanfare in which all the basses and drums join loudly, an obese bishop who appears ready to burst, a Punch-and-Judy magistrate, coquettes, a kind of Diafoirus (a quack doctor described by Molière) in a high peaked hat, bourgois figures, fishwives, a Lancer wearing a shako, a couple of lovers kissing, more masks, clowns, a skeleton in an opera hat. Meanwhile flags are hanging from the fronts of buildings, while curious onlookers cluster on balconies and at windows, and on a raised platform a barker and clowns temporarily suspend their spiel and sideshow to gape at the thousands of people, the most distant ones appearing no larger than pinheads. It is an epical satirical scene, full of humor and burlesque details, conscious anachronisms and surprising inventions, and from it pours in a flood an aura of health, good humor, gaiety, the whole accompanied by what sounds like a gust of hearty laughter! «One of the greatest artistic creations of our time,» declared André de Ridder in a respectful tribute. In any case, it is one of the most remarquable examples of Expressionism.

Ensor more than any other artist is the true embodiment of Flemish Expressionism. He was the precursor rather than the real founder of the movement, without intending to be or even realizing it, for the least of his concerns was founding a school. From the very first he lifted the movement to a level which it has not surpassed since. His name comes automatically to lips or pen, and invariably leads the list, when art historians cite the adherents of an artistic movement in which were involved painters such as Henri Evenepoel, Gustave de Smet, Edgar Tytgat, Frits Van den Berghe, Albert Servaes, and Constant Permeke.

Beginning in 1886, Ensor, a complete and unusual artist, capable of working in very many different styles and of employing every possible technique, decided to devote part of his time to engraving. And his engravings alone would be enough to establish his reputation. The catalogue of his etchings and drypoints, compiled by Albert Croquez, contains no less than a hundred and thirty-three entries (plus an album of thirty-two lithographs). Some of them have been enhanced by watercolor or colored pencils.

Ensor enjoyed using his burin to depict a wide range of subjects, poetic, fantastic, satirical, even pseudohistorical. In these prints, perhaps even more than in his painted works, he demonstrates an outpouring of creative power, notable for its verse, always straightforward, and occasionally ferocious. What André de Ridder called Ensor's «gift of mockery» is displayed in his satirical works: *Winds* (1888), *Plague Here, Plague There, Plague Everywhere* (1888) (see p. 80), *Demons Teasing Me* (1888) (see p. 59), *The Exterminating Angel* (1889), the series of *The Seven Deadly Sins* (1902–1904) (see pp. 82, 83). Anyone who examines them carefully will discover a wealth of provocative details and droll items: *Fight of the Demons* or *Devils Thrashing*

STILL LIFE WITH PEACHES, 1890 Oil on canvas, $7^1/_2''$ × $9^7/_{16}''$ (19 × 24 cm.)
Collection: Marcel Mabille, Brussels

THE INTRIGUE, 1890   Oil on canvas, 35⁷/₁₆″ × 59¹/₁₆″ (90 × 150 cm.)
Koninklijk Museum voor Schone Kunsten, Antwerp

64

◁
A Cross Face, 1890
Oil on canvas, 9⅝″ × 7½″ (24,5 × 19 cm.)
Collection: Marcel Mabille, Brussels

Masks (Skeletons) Fighting for the Body
of a Hanged Man, 1891
Oil on canvas, 23¼″ × 29⅛″ (59 × 74 cm.)
Koninklijk Museum voor Schone Kunsten, Antwerp

65

STILL LIFE WITH BLUE PITCHER, 1890–91
Oil on panel, 14¾″ × 18″ (37,5 × 45,6 cm.)   Staatsgalerie, Stuttgart

STILL LIFE WITH RAY, 1892   Oil on canvas, $31\frac{1}{2}'' \times 39\frac{3}{8}''$ (80 $\times$100 cm.)
Musées Royaux des Beaux-Arts de Belgique, Brussels

CHRIST CALMING THE STORM, 1891   Oil on canvas, 31½″ × 39⅜″ (80 × 100 cm.)
Stedelijk Museum, Ostend

Christ Calming the Storm, 1886   Drypoint and etching, 6" × 9⅛" (15,3 × 23 cm.)
Collection: Mr. and Mrs. Herman D. Shickman

Angels and Archangels (1888) (see p. 43), *Battle of the Golden Spurs* (1895) (see p. 74) and *The Baths at Ostend* (1899) (see p. 75). A typical instance: Ensor depicted Lady Godiva in the nude, which was an accurate representation, but endowed with voluptuous curves and seen from the back, galloping through the streets of Coventry clinging to the neck of her mount, so that her derrière, raised up out of the saddle, and the hindquarters of the horse superimpose their magnificent rotundities in a thoroughly comical manner.

What a contrast, thanks to the author's rich imagination, to *Scenes from the Life of Christ* and a host of pure and balanced landscapes: *Grand View of Mariakerke* (1887) (see p. 27), *The Harbor of Ostend* (1888) (see p. 39), *A Gust of Wind at the Edge of the Forest* (1888) (see p. 8), *The Pool of Poplars* (1889), *Farm at Leffinghe* (1889), and *The Beach at La Panne* (1904). Nor should we overlook the amazing *Portrait of Ernest Rousseau* (1887) (see p. 23), which Louis Lebeer described as a «masterpiece of perceptiveness and boldness of technique.»

Ensor's burin brings to life the great movements of crowds, which he excels in drawing, as well as some movie directors: *The Cathedral* (1891) (see p. 19), *Battle of Waterloo* (1891), *The Multiplication of the Fishes* (1891) (see p. 57), and *Death Chasing the Flock of Mortals* (1896). Occasionally, several years after the originals, he repeated subjects which he had treated

The Wicked Physicians, 1895 Etching, 6¾" × 9¾" (17,2 × 24,6 cm.)
Art Institute of Chicago. Print and Drawing Fund

earlier, such as *Sick Tramp Warming Himself* (1895). At other times, following a reverse pattern, his brush took up the torch passed on by his burin, as in *Boats Aground* (1888).

«Another Callot,» Paul Haesaerts called him. His prints are admirable for the purity and simplicity of the lines, the lightness of touch, the feeling for composition. The most remarkable aspect is the fact that an artist so enamored of light should have been able to depict the play of light in black and white. «One could argue that light as depicted by Ensor could not conceivably be reproduced except through the shimmering play of colors,» observed Louis Lebeer, «if the painter had not proved, in his etchings and his drypoints, that he needed only a few lines, indeed a few dots, to capture the very essence of that light and its effect on figures and objects.»

A unique and innovative genius, Ensor did not belong to any school. He was an advocate of the unencumbered by rigid rules, the creator of works which were pure poetry. «Reason,» he said, «is the enemy of Art.» A nonconformist, he was answerable only to himself and obeyed only his own impulses. One should recognize in his flights of fancy not only an effort to break with reality or demonstrate a taste for farce, but, essentially, the impetuous outbursts of an

The Good Judges, 1894   Etching, 7⅛″ × 9⅜″ (18 × 23,9 cm.)
Art Institute of Chicago. Print and Drawing Fund

artist eager to try everything. Paul Haesaerts described him as « a great adventurer, a daredevil of the art world, one of the most audacious men in the history of painting. »

THE DARK YEARS

A truly independent artist and a liberated man, he had to pay a high price for being such a maverick!

It is not enough to paint and to accumulate canvases. One must exhibit, become known, sell them in order to live. And that was where Ensor began to experience disappointment and frustration. His painting was too far removed from the beaten path not to be shocking to his contemporaries, who were inclined to admire the fussily polished paintings of the disciples of David, especially the work of the Belgian Navez. The Salons disdainfully rejected the pictures Ensor submitted to them. And if a few artistic groups agreed to let him show his art in their exhibitions, it was on condition that he agree to eliminate some of his most typical works.

71

At the same time, those young artists who were tired of having doors shut in their faces because they had dared break with the academic tradition were becoming more numerous. In 1883, in Brussels, writer Gustave Maus founded «Les Vingt» (Twenty), an avant-garde movement that accepted the task of making known and defending innovative artists. Among them were painters Van Rysselberghe, Khnopff, Van Strydonck, Vogels, Ensor, and a few others. It is that moment that masks the start of the «struggles for art,» a battle in the forefront of which Ensor would be fighting.

The first exhibition of «Les Vingt» took place in 1884. Ensor showed six canvases. They caused an enormous sensation! Of all of the exhibitors, the man of Ostend was the last to find favor in the eyes of the public. Confronted by his pictures, the visitors to the show bristled. Some of them appeared to be horrified, as if they were seeing an obscene show. Others were content to greet the pictures with a sneer. Indignant and sarcastic protests multiplied. «His pictures are certainly among those which have had to listen to the most stupid remarks,» sighed Demolder.

As to the critics, one might ask, what did they think of Ensor? Nothing very complimentary either. «His *Woman Eating Oysters* and his *Bouquet of Poppies* are truly two examples of street-fair art,» was the conclusion of «The Gazette.» If, in the beginning, these gentlemen showed a little restraint in judging him, it was only because he disconcerted them by «disregarding completely the pictorial proprieties,» as one of them noted. Later on, led by the great pundits Fétis and Sulzberger, they no longer showed the same self-control, but dipped their pens in vitriol each time that they had to review the exhibitions of their «bête noire.» To a man the Belgian press exploded in a violent reaction against his works. Their individual venoms united until there was a veritable cabal opposing him. The unfortunate man was fiercely attacked; sarcastic comments and insults were systematically heaped on him. «Ignoble sights!» one journalist wrote about his canvases. «Sinister idiocies!» said another. «Sickening studio rubbish!» exclaimed a third. And still another went them one better with: «That is painting? No way! It is garbage!» The critic who was satisfied to speak of «shapeless studies, painful and sad,» sounded like a moderate.

«A hail of cruel comments is falling on my head,» Ensor wrote. «They are abusing me, insulting me; I am mad, I am stupid, I am wicked, bad, incapable, ignorant!» It is true that at this same time Belgian critics were using the words «clowns,» «hoaxers,» and «neurotics» to describe Pissarro, Renoir, and Van Gogh. Ensor avenged himself on these «pretentious know-nothings ... swallowing rustry old coins,» by depicting, in *Ecce Homo,* or *Christ and the Critics* (1891), Christ with a rope around his neck and wearing a crown of thorns, flanked by his executioners, the critics Fétis and Sulzberger.

In view of the fact that the artist was confronted along the road with so many diatribes, that to quote Verhaeren he had to endure «the cutting edge of stupidity,» and that he was «crushed, bruised and wounded» by the blows he suffered, he must be forgiven the excess of bad humor and the excesses of his pen when, at moments when he found his patience tried, he let himself go and sounded off in magazine articles. The pithily pointed turns of phrase which he invneted, high-sounding, full of imagery, packed with alliterations and assonances, with strings of epithets, farfetched and sometimes invented expressions, added to the corrosive effect. «Demolition experts with suckers,» he said of those who did not like him and whose sentiments he reciprocated, «octopuses crawling on a surface of sand, spiders with mustaches, silky ruffians ...»

A more serious fact was that those who might be expected to share his opinions did not understand him any better. His colleagues were convinced that he had gone astray. A number of his comrades in «Les Vingt,» beginning with Maus, «the Mandarin,» who reproached him for turning his back on Realism, concluded that his style was exaggerated and preposterous and that his excesses risked jeopardizing the cause of the independent artists. On a number of occasions Ensor was formally requested to exclude from the pictures he was submitting some that were thought to be unnecessarily scandalous and outspoken. Twice, every picture which he submitted was rejected. His exclusion was put to a vote. And this was supposedly an innovative and audacious movement! «The most advanced in the world,» in the opinion of Alfred Barr. In spite of this «vexatious lack of understanding,» Ensor clung to «Les Vingt» until the group disbanded in 1893, for he realized that he would not be permitted to exhibit anywhere else. «Someone who

GARDEN OF LOVE, 1891   Oil on canvas, 31½″ × 39″ (80 × 99 cm.)
Collection: Louis Franck, Esq., C.B.E. Gstaad

Battle of the Golden Spurs, 1895   Etching, 6¾" × 9⅜" (17,3 × 23,7 cm.)
Collection: Mrs. Barbara Meyer Elesh

has not been understood up to this very day,» Eugène Demolder said of him in 1892, «one of those larger-than-life fellows of such limitless originality that at times the crowd howled in protest against his canvases like a pack of starving dogs upset by an unaccustomed star.»

Selling his works was out of the question. In 1889, his *Afternoon at Ostend* was put on sale in the Kursaal at the price of 350 francs. At the end of the season not a single buyer had appeared. Then, in a show of bravado, Ensor took down the canvas and made a rug of it. When, in 1893, in a fit of depression, he offered the entire lot of the pictures stacked in his studio for the sum total of only 8 500 francs, no one availed himself of the offer. At times, if he wished to paint new pictures, the lack of money forced him to use canvases that had already been painted on. There were moments when, overcome by despair, he lost heart, abandoned his easel, and gave way to tears. «I am not understood!» he exclaimed one day to Emma Lambotte, a friend. «I shall be obliged to throw away palette and brushes, give up painting and become a seashell salesman!»

*The Baths at Ostend, 1899   Etching, hand colored, 8⅜″ × 10⅝″ (21,3 × 26,8 cm.)
Art Institute of Chicago. Gift from the estate of Curt Valentin*

It would be an exaggeration to call him an accursed painter, but during the long years he was an artistic outcast, the most creative years of his life, he was willing to live on the «ragged edge» rather than relinquish his art. In fact, Ensor took refuge in a dream universe in which the plays of color emanating from his imagination consoled him for his disappointment and frustration. Overflowing with vitality, given to sardonic outbursts, biting irony, and mystifying humor, it was by exercising these characteristics that he showed himself to be prodigiously inventive.

In his masquerades he appears to be having fun. In reality, hurt by his failures, he was discouraged and distressed. Scornful, sarcastic, unfathomable, he put a mask over his own visage so that what he felt could not be seen. He expressed his feelings openly only through his work. More than merely a game or show of defiance; it was a protest, a rebellious outcry, an anguished complaint.

The people of Ostend did not take long to recognize that they had among them an artistic pariah. Without understanding exactly what was the matter, they saw in him, as his young friend

76 GARDEN OF LOVE, 1895   Watercolor and mixed media, 5½″ × 4¼″ (14 × 10,8 cm.)
Collection: Mr. and Mrs. James W. Alsdorf, Chicago

Hop Frog's Revenge, 1898   Etching, hand colored, 13¾″ × 9½″ (35 × 24,2 cm.)
Art Institute of Chicago. Wrenn Memorial Collection of Prints

REMORSE OF THE
CORSICAN OGRE, 1891
Oil on canvas,
6¼″ × 8½″
(16 × 21,5 cm.)
Collection:
Marcel Mabille,
Brussels

ENSOR AND GENERAL
LÉMAN DISCUSS
PAINTING, 1890
Oil on canvas,
4¾″ × 6¼″
(12 × 16 cm.)
Collection:
Marcel Mabille,
Brussels

GROTESQUE SINGERS,
1891
Oil on canvas,
6¼″ × 8½″
(16 × 21,6 cm.)
Collection:
Marcel Mabille,
Brussels

MADEMOISELLE
DEMOLDER
IN BULLFIGHTERS'
APPAREL, 1895
Watercolor,
10⁷/₁₆″ × 13³/₈″
(26,5 × 34 cm.)
Collection:
Marcel Mabille,
Brussels

Plague Here, Plague There, Plague Everywhere, 1888   Pencil and red chalk, 8⅝″ × 11⅞″ (22 × 30 cm.)
Koninklijk Museum voor Schone Kunsten, Antwerp

Jean-Jacques Gaillard said, «a kind of crazy person who enjoyed causing a sensation.» They kept
their distance from the painter and whispered when he passed by. On carnival evenings groups
of maskers stood under his window to give him mock serenades, and looking at these noisy and
tumultuous masked bands, one could easily imagine that they were characters who had stepped
out of his canvases, rebelling against their creator, and were teasing him.

   What is more, everything helped enhance his reputation as a shady character. Gossip spread
like a whirlwind. People recounted how one day Ensor's father, fully clothed, had plunged from
the stockade and swum across the channel . . . that Ensor's mother was an ill-tempered shrew
and that she even double-locked her door to keep her husband at home and prevent him from
seeking to drink himself into oblivion . . . that his Aunt Mimi was accustomed to playing the piano
late at night with all the windows open, and that she had been seen taking a walk on the sea dike,
her canary cage in her hand, so that the bird could have a breath of fresh air . . . that Mitche, the
painter's sister, had married a Chinese, and that on their wedding day both of them were dressed
in the style of the Celestial Empire . . . that Ensor, for his part, amused himself by teasing the
fishwives in the market, and that the latter responded to his gibes by insulting him and throwing
fish at his head. . . . Indeed, what did they not say! . . .

PORTRAIT OF
EUGÈNE DEMOLDER,
1893
Oil on canvas,
14⅛″ × 8¼″
(36 × 21 cm.)
Collection:
Marcel Mabille,
Brussels

Gluttony, 1902.
From the
«Seven Deadly Sins»
Drawing,
3¹⁵/₁₆″ × 5⁵/₁₆″
(10 × 13,5 cm.)
Collection:
Louis Franck, Esq.,
C.B.E. Gstaad

Avarice, 1902.
From the
«Seven Deadly Sins»
Drawing,
3¹⁵/₁₆″ × 5⁵/₁₆″
(10 × 13,5 cm.)
Collection:
Louis Franck, Esq.,
C.B.E. Gstaad

Sloth, 1900.
From the
«Seven Deadly Sins»
Drawing,
$3^{15}/_{16}'' \times 5^1/_2''$
(10 × 14 cm.)
Collection:
Louis Franck, Esq.,
C.B.E. Gstaad

Anger, 1902.
From the
«Seven Deadly Sins»
Drawing,
$3^5/_{16}'' \times 5^1/_2''$
(9,5 × 14 cm.)
Collection:
Louis Franck, Esq.,
C.B.E. Gstaad

MASKS AND DEATH, 1897
Oil on canvas, 31⅛″ × 39⅜″ (79 × 100 cm.)
Musée des Beaux-Arts, Liège

▷

SKELETONS WARMING THEMSELVES, 1895
Etching, hand colored, 5¹/₁₆″ × 4″ (13,9 × 10,2 cm.)
Gallery Le Bateau-Lavoir, Paris

Skeletons Playing Billiards, 1903   Drawing, 9⁷/₁₆″ × 11¹³/₁₆″ (24 × 30 cm.)
Collection: Marcel Mabille, Brussels

Ensor found neither understanding nor support in his family. Only his father approved of him. His mother, his grandmother, and his aunt, cold and calculating bourgeoises who thought solely in terms of money, held it against him that he wasted his time daubing canvases which no one wanted when he could have had a fine position in the world of trade. The family, shaken by domestic storms, was deadlocked in conflict.

The captive of an art that did not give him financial independence, imprisoned within the confines of a narrow milieu where his best years were wasted, crushed under the weight of dissatisfaction with the provincial society of his day, Ensor suffered from the dullness of his existence. «I am dying,» he exclaimed. «I am being drowned in platitudes, rotted by a wicked lack of kindness and dull monotony!» When he could no longer endure having his soul squeezed as if by vise, he quickly boarded the train to Brussels.

Mirror with Skeletons, 1890   Drawing, 11¹³/₁₆″ × 8⁵/₈″ (30 × 22 cm.)   Collection: Marcel Mabille, Brussels

OUR TWO PORTRAITS, 1905   Oil on canvas, 16⅛″ × 13″ (41 × 33 cm.)
Collection: Marcel Mabille, Brussels

In the capital he was offered refuge in a friendly household, the home of the Rousseau family on Rue Vautier. Ernest Rousseau, a professor of physics and rector of the University of Brussels, was a man of science, cultured, good-hearted, tolerant, with a sense of humor. His wife Mariette loved beauty and respected new ideas. Both enveloped the painter in an aura of sympathetic understanding, particularly Mariette, his « good genius. » She comforted him when he was beset by doubts and discouraged, and from time to time bought a canvas. The son of the house, Pierre, a medical student, was his best friend, a veritable brother. In the bosom of what he called « his second family, » Ensor could breathe freely, achieve serenity, and find new reasons to struggle and to hope.

A niece of the Rousseaus, Blanche Rousseau, has described their first meeting. « I can see again that tall figure, dressed in black and ghastly pale, standing in a dark corner, making a hesitant gesture with an elegant hand that was tentatively extended toward us — and above all, the rapid and searching glance of his darting eyes, his extraordinary eyes, shy, provocative, gentle, sarcastic and evasive, quickly looking up and down while his great stiff body bent awkwardly. He had the face of a mocking Christ or of a melancholy Satan. He spoke of the devil in a low voice. »

In Ostend the only sweetness in his solitary existence was provided by a woman, who had to meet him clandestinely. She was Augusta Boogaerts, whom he nicknamed « the Siren, » the daughter of a innkeeper of the city who had come to work at the souvenir shop as a salesgirl. Ten years younger than Ensor, she was charming and lively, with an ironic turn of mind. But was she capable of understanding the tall, slightly mad young man who, in her arms, let himself dream impossible dreams? She wanted to marry him, but Ensor's parents opposed the idea. There began a quiet struggle between them. For his part, the painter stayed aloof from the battle. Nevertheless she remained faithful to him. Their long liaison would not come to an end until the death of the painter. Augusta, eighty years old by then, the illicit Baucis of a Philomenon who balked at wedlock, survived him by barely a year.

This romance of sixty years' duration is recalled in a curious picture in which both of the lovers are portrayed, but separately as if they wished to be discreet, she in the foreground, he slightly to the rear: *Our Two Portraits* (see p. 88). But apart from this one painting, nothing that throws any light on Ensor's love life is revealed in his pictures. Only a few nude women can be found on his canvases, and they assuredly do not reflect the brilliance of Venus, for they are not the sort of sensual and disturbing nudes on which men's eyes tend to linger caressingly. The female body does not play a large part in Ensor's pictures and prints. With a few exceptions it figures only in a subsidiary and secondary role or else as an element in caricature. However, Firmin Cuypers noted that there were some erotic cartoons, dating from 1918 on, that the painter showed to no one. « Every kind of sexual game, » he reported, « games of the flesh and games of pleasure, is on display in scenes both voluptuous and lecherous, which Ensor's libido endows with a steamy sensuality. » Paul Haesaerts supplied the additional information that these little drawings were destroyed « by sacrilegious hands. »

ASCENT TO THE SUMMIT

Yet in spite of everything, not everybody treated Ensor with contempt. He was also blessed with several enthusiastic admirers who were indignant at seeing his genius scoffed at and misunderstood. These were young Belgian writers such as Verhaeren, Edmond Picard, Maeterlinck, Georges Eeckhoud and, above all, Eugène Demolder, his most dedicated supporter and the most determined to win respect for him. « It was the writers who, in the last analysis, won Ensor's battle for him, » Firmin Cuypers affirmed categorically.

The reputation that he was finally able to achieve through their efforts and that he was unable to enjoy until he was about forty was at the beginning a reputation limited to a small circle of devotees. Only the small periodicals bestowed guarded praise on him, while the large papers continued to vilify him. Although he received publicity in France through a special issue of the Parisian magazine, «La Plume», he was still unknown in his own country. His one-man exhibitions, the first of which took place in Brussels in 1896 and the second of which was in Paris, won him only a few additional admirers. As to buyers, he found only a meager number of enlightened Maecenases, including François Franck, «the good Lord of contemporary art,» who was for him «the greatest of patrons.» Thanks to Franck, «the seven fat cows bearing the seven deadly sins augured very well indeed.» Also thanks to him, the Museum of Antwerp possesses now the finest collection of Ensor's works that can be seen anywhere. The Museum of Brussels finally agreed to acquire a canvas by Ensor in 1896. Selecting from among those generally considered the least provocative, it chose *The Lamp Boy.*

Gradually, however, the wall of incomprehension that had been erected around the painter of masks cracked and crumbled. People began to do him justice, to see in his work something besides lunacy and sensationalism. In 1901 he was among the founding members of the Free Academy of Belgium. Two years later he was made a «Chevalier» of the Order of Leopold. Monographs about him were written, the earliest one by his friend Demolder.

Yet just at the moment his «crystalline period» began — a period whose characteristics, according to Paul Haesaerts, were fluid colors, tones at once lively and blurred, wavering lines, and the absence of any internal structure — a weariness became apparent in the works produced by Ensor. He would still paint pictures magnificently vigorous and bold, but they would be exceptions rather than the rule: *Hop-Frog's Revenge* (c. 1910) (see the hand colored etching p. 77), *The Deliverance of Andromeda* (1925), *Port of Ostend* (1933), and *Ensor at the Harmonium* (1933). In the other paintings one can no longer find the same vitality and the same originality. Instead there are traces of fatigue, hesitancy, and ineffectiveness.

Ensor's creative inspiration weakened and his technique deteriorated. At the age of forty the artist of Ostend had said all he had to say, had done everything. He had produced the major part of his work, had exhausted through repetition the vigorous, fresh, and innovative statements he wished to make. Nothing that he painted thereafter would add a penny's worth to his glory. He would simply repeat himself, copy himself, plagiarize himself, sometimes predating his canvases so that they could command a better price. Paradoxically, honors were heaped upon him at the very time when, having executed his most undeniable masterpieces, his talent was flagging.

This decline, which came prematurely at what should have been the prime of his life, undoubtedly had a psychological basis. The attacks he had endured, the long struggle sustained without any respite, the failures, the bitterness, the grief — all of these had shattered something in Ensor's soul. Even his literary style, formerly so formidable, became less sharp as his rancor diminished. His penned blows no longer even scratched. «Ensor,» said Grégoire Le Roy, «now fights with a buttoned foil.» Without bitterness and also without malice, the painter seemed to sink into a state of blissful indifference.

Thanks to the ferment of intellectual fever inspired by the postwar period, it was from 1920 on that Ensor's reputation flourished. Studies devoted to his art multiplied. Retrospectives of his art were organized in Brussels and Antwerp. In 1932 Paris gave his pictures, which were exhibited at the Musée du Jeu de Paume, its nod of approval. His other exhibitions, in Paris again in 1939, in Dresden, in Basel, in Venice, in Florence, in Rotterdam, in Hannover, and in London, were equally successful. His canvases, his drawings, his etchings had numerous devout admirers. Museums and private collectors vied with one another to acquire his works. The prices obtained for everything and anything which bore the painter's signature were among the highest ever paid in Belgium for the pictures of a living artist. «A reaction is taking place,» Ensor acknowledged ironically, «the exceptional and hitherto unacceptable painter is now being praised by frenetic fans.»

Honors were showered upon the master. In 1925 he was admitted into the Royal Academy of Belgium. In 1929 King Albert made him a baron in spite of the opposition of some members of the Heraldic Council, who were not disposed to accept the son of shopkeepers as a member of the nobility. Two years later his bust, chiselled by Edmond de Valeriola, was installed in a square of

Ostend. That same year the Antwerp composer Flor Alpaerts composed a « James Ensor Suite.» In 1933 Ensor's colleagues proclaimed him to be the «prince of painters.» A French cabinet minister, Anatole de Monzie, journeyed to Ostend for the express purpose of bestowing on him the decoration of the Legion of Honor. Thus was he « stunned under a hail of powerful blows from the incense snuffer!»

If he blazed a trail for innovative artists, nevertheless there were none who followed directly in his footsteps. Yet numerous Flemish painters — De Smet, Tytgat, Permeke, Rik Wouters — declared themselves to be his disciples, while a number of foreign artists — Chagall, the German Nolde, the Dutchman Toorop — acknowledge his influence. The critics, wary and distrustful, ended by belatedly keeping step with public opinion, which by then was unanimously enthusiastic about the Ostend artist. He was seen to be «one of the initiators of contemporary nonrealistic art, the prophetic precursor of Expressionism and Surrealism.» In Belgium he was respected as a national idol. The man who for so long had been disparaged, ridiculed, and put to shame was suddenly hailed as the greatest painter his country had produced since Rubens and Van Dyck. He was called «the father of twentieth-century Belgian painting.» An Association of the Friends of Ensor was formed under the sponsorship of Queen Elizabeth. What an about-face! How much ground had been covered since the exhibitions of «Les Vingt.»

Having become an elderly gentleman with a snowy-white beard and hair, honored, feted, adulated like no one else, decorated, made a nobleman, immortalized in sculpture, treated as an illustrious artist, but no longer concentrating on his work, surprised by the favorable reception it was belatedly receiving and skeptical as to the sincerity of the praise heaped on it, Ensor's attitude was one of mockery as he climbed the heights to the summit. His unexpected glory did not turn his head. With his customary irony he gently made fun of himself: «Here is an old man, his hair grown white under the harness, bending beneath the yoke of excessive homage.»

From 1917 on Ensor lived in a house inherited from an uncle, also a souvenir merchant, located at number 17 (that today is 27), rue de Flandre, which, terminating in a ramp, opens directly onto the sea and seems to ascend toward the sky. (1) He kept the shop on the ground floor, not allowing it to be used for business. Upstairs he set up a parlor-studio that replaced his attic. He spent most of his time there in the midst of his fetishes — an unlikely collection of Chinese curios, silks of faded colors from the Orient, seashells, pieces of coral, fans whose folds were torn, curiosities such as an alleged mermaid, entirely fabricated naturally, and, of course, masks — all of which contrasted sharply with the lavender wallpaper and were reflected in the glass globe attached to the chandelier. One visitor noted that it was, when «taken in detail, ugly and in what could be called poor taste; taken as a whole, what beauty!»

Among all this bric-à-brac, the warm tones of some of the master's favorite canvases blare out like a fanfare. They include *Self-Portrait in a Flowered Hat,* which he would never agree to give up, and *The Entry of Christ into Brussels,* an immense fresco that, when featured in an exhibition, had to be carried out of the studio through the French windows, over a dismantled balcony.

It was here that Ensor, affable, simple, a mischievous smile playing behind his white beard, received the legion of his visitors — some of them famous, such as Einstein — attracted by his fame and his legend. His bright eyes revealed flashes of mischievousness when they witnessed the visitors' surprise and wonder. He permitted them to explore portfolios crammed full of drawings. With a practiced finger he strummed for them on the harmonium sparkling, light music that he had composed for *The Scale of Love,* a ballet-pantomine in one act for which he also wrote the libretto and designed the sets. And he never failed to confess that he was convinced that he had taken the wrong road and that he should have devoted himself to music. Or else he had them listen to one of his recorded talks. Or perhaps he read them a few selected pages from his «Writings,» just as he did at the banquets given in his honor when with the dessert he would recite doggerel verses in his own way.

---

(1) This house has since been converted into an Ensor Museum.

Nymphs in Movement, 1926   Oil on canvas, 39″ × 43⁵⁄₁₆″ (99 × 110 cm.)   Private collection

Clearsighted, he was well aware of the deterioration of his talent. He would not have picked up a brush again if his entourage, excited by his success, had not urged him to do so. The «Siren» was determined to make him work. Taking advantage of her influence with him, she set up still life compositions before which she seated the painter, palette in hand. She supervised his production of pictures and engravings, kept an inventory, and attended to their sale. This assertion of authority inevitably led to some clashes between the two. One day, about to go out and knowing that she was due to return, Ensor left on the table a note intended for her, «Do not take anything; I have counted everything.» On his return, he found an equally laconic note, «Do not count anything; I have taken everything.»

Eventually he yielded to the tranquillity of provincial life. Adoring them both equally, he paid joint tribute to Ostend and the sea, «Ostend, fairy ruler of the heavens and the multicolored waters! — Ostend, queen of the capricious sea, queen of the soft sands and of the heavens heavy with gold and opal!» His one great regret was that he had failed to prevent the destruction and the despoiling which had caused so much damage to the town and the dunes. Heaven knows to what extent these crimes against the beauty of nature and the environment aroused his indignation and his anger!

«A kind of Victor Hugo, bemedaled and content,» he was called by Michel Ragon. An erect and sturdy septuagenarian, dressed in black, a cape thrown over his shoulders, he could be seen walking on the beach and over the dunes. Even when the bombardments of 1940 took place, nothing could induce him to move from the Rue de Flandre.

Very feeble, he spent the last years of his life confined to the mezzanine of his house, seated in front of the window, his mental faculties dulled, his arm joint stiff, a hat clamped down on his head lest he feel a draft, cared for by a vigilant and surly domestic. When he was almost ninety, he expired peacefully at dawn on November 19, 1949, after an illness which had lasted three weeks.

His death caused an immense stir throughout the artistic world. He was given a regal burial. Nothing was lacking — a military fanfare, flags, a long tolling of bells sounding a death knell. Cabinet ministers, generals, judges, bishops, the great names of art and literature — everyone of those whom he had made fun of throughout his life — rushed to pay his last respects to a «great personage who brought honor to Belgium,» as the papers reported. There were funeral services which would almost certainly have caused the Baron Ensor to smile. Buried in the little cemetery of Notre-Dame des Dunes, in Mariakerke, he sleeps the last sleep facing the sea he so loved.

«The place of James Ensor in the artistic history of his time seems both clear and distinguished,» Emile Verhaeren wrote as early as 1908. And indeed posterity has proven the poet right. Ensor? «A prototype of the imaginative and fanciful artist,» is how Paul Haesaerts described him. Jean Cassou saw in him «one of the greatest artists, one of the greatest visionaries of all time.» Alfred Barr and William Lieberman called him «the grand master of the imagination.» «One of the greatest painters produced by the modern Western world,» was the judgment of Paul Fierens. And Frank Edebau saluted him as «the brilliant artist and the pioneer who, starting as an exponent of realistic Impressionism, within a few years created a style so personal that he opened to art paths whose existence had not been suspected until then — the very paths which led directly to Expressionism, to Fauvism, to Surrealism, indeed to the very threshold of the artistic movement of today.»

There was nothing either classical or rational in the style of the man who called himself «painter of masks and of the sea,» but rather a taste for the bizarre, a very personal vision, and the determination to create a new sort of art. Paul Fierens accurately defined the resulting work as, «light and airy world in which matter takes second place, in which color is transformed into spirit, in which poetry surges from all sides, from the commonplace as well as from the unusual.»

One day Ensor confided to a friend: «I wish to survive, and for a long time in the future to speak to the men of tomorrow.» This supreme ambition is realized from beyond the grave. Through his works, James Ensor continues to live, to speak, to smile ironically.

Perhaps, after all, the smile on the face with such a melancholy expression was also a mask.

BIOGRAPHY

1860 On April 13, in Ostend, James Sidney Ensor was born, the son of Frédéric James Ensor and Maria Catharina Haegheman.

1873 Admitted to the Collège Notre-Dame in Ostend.

1877 Admitted to the Académie des Beaux-Arts in Brussels.

1880 Returned to Ostend and established a permanent residence there.

1881 For the first time exhibited in a show, the exhibition of the group «La Chrysalide» (The Chrysalis), in Brussels.

1883 Exhibited in show of «L'Essor» (The Flight). Octave Maus founded the group known as «Les Vingt» (The XX). Ensor became a member.

1884 All the canvases submitted by Ensor to the Salon of Brussels were rejected. The first articles on Ensor were published in periodicals.

1888 Start ,of Ensor's long liaison with Augusta Boogaerts.

1892 Publication of the first monograph devoted to Ensor, written by Eugène Demolder.

1893 «Les Vingt» broke up.

1896 First one-man show of Ensor's work in Brussels. First acquisition of one his paintings (*The Lamp Boy*) by a museum, the Museum of Brussels.

1898 An Ensor exhibition in Paris, organized by the periodical, «La Plume».

1899 Special issue of «La Plume» devoted to Ensor.

1901 Edmond Picard founded the Free Academy of Brussels. Ensor was one of the founding members.

1903 Awarded the Order of Leopold.

1920 Fist retrospective exhibition, organized by the Giroux Gallery in Brussels.

1921 Retrospective exhibition in Antwerp. Publication of the first volume of the «Writings of James Ensor».

1926 Exhibited in Paris and at the Biennale in Venice.

1927 Exhibition in Hannover.

1929 Exhibition at the Palais des Beaux-Arts in Brussels. Ensor was made a baron.

1931 The unveiling in Ostend of a bust of Ensor.

1932 Exhibition in Paris, at the Musée du Jeu de Paume.

1933 Prince of painters. Awarded the Legion of Honor.

1939 Exhibition in Paris.

1946 Retrospective exhibition at the National Gallery, London.

1949 Ensor died on November 19, at the age of 89. Buried in Mariakerke.

BIBLIOGRAPHY

WRITINGS OF JAMES ENSOR

Les Ecus. Ill. with 14 colored line drawings. Ostend, G. Daveluy, 1904.

Les Ecrits de James Ensor. Ill. with 35 line drawings. Brussels, Sélection, 1921.

La Gamme d'amour. Text and music, with color ill. Brussels, Un Coup de Dés, 1929.

Les Ecrits de James Ensor. (1928–1934). Antwerp, L'Art contemporain, 1934.

Les Ecrits de James Ensor. Foreword by Henri Vandeputte. Final edition. Reproduction of 32 original drawings. Brussels, Edition Lumière, 1944.

Lettres à André De Ridder. Antwerp, Librairie des Arts, 1960.